392.5
Mayled
Marriage Customs

DATE DUE			

Religious Topics

MARRIAGE CUSTOMS

Jon Mayled

Silver Burdett Press
Morristown, N.J.

Religious Topics

Birth Customs   Initiation Rites
Death Customs   Marriage Customs
Feasting and Fasting   Pilgrimage

First published in 1986 by Wayland (Publishers) Limited
61 Western Road, Hove, East Sussex, England BN3 1JD

Adapted and first published in the United States in 1987 by
Silver Burdett Press, Morristown, New Jersey.

Library of Congress Cataloging-in-Publication Data

Mayled, Jon.
    Marriage customs.

    (Religious topics)
    Bibliography: p.
    Includes index.
    Summary: Describes how marriages are celebrated by Buddhists,
Christians, Jews, Muslims, and members of other religions.
    1. Marriage customs and rites – Juvenile literature. [1. Marriage
customs and rites]
I. Title   II. Series.
GT2665.M38   1987   392′.5   86–31469
ISBN 0–382–09448–4

Phototypeset by Kalligraphics Limited, Redhill, Surrey, England
Printed by Casterman, S.A., Belgium

Contents

Introduction

Some marriage services can be very eleborate, as is this ceremony in Malaya.

For many people their marriage, or wedding, is one of the most important events in their lives. In all religions, it means that a man and a woman tell their friends and relatives that from now on they want to live with each other. If a girl has been living with her parents, she will leave their home and live with her new husband. Often the marriage is performed by the leader of the couple's religious group. During the service, they make a promise to the God or gods of their religion that they will look after each other and stay together for the rest of their lives. They also ask their God or gods to bless them and help them.

You will see that in many religions great care is taken by the families of the couple to make sure they will be happy together. Because a secure home and family life are vital, families hope the newly married couple will be good and responsible parents toward any children they may have.

Marriage ceremonies are always followed by a party. This is a Hindu celebration.

Buddhism

For Buddhists, the way in which a marriage takes place varies according to the country in which the couple live and which tradition of the religion they follow. Buddhists of Thailand, for example, are of the *Theravada* school. However, wherever people are married, the Buddhist monks (*Sangha*) always play a part.

Before the wedding takes place, a monk usually checks the horoscopes (the star signs) of the couple to make sure they will get along with each other, and to choose the best day for the ceremony.

In Thailand the marriage does not take place in a temple or church but in a hall or hotel. The bride and the bridegroom wear special clothes embroidered with silk, and sit

The Buddhist couple sit with their sponsors in front of the Sangha.

Flowers play a part in the marriage ceremony of this Buddhist couple from Thailand.

side by side on silk cushions. Next to them sit another Buddhist couple, the sponsors of the couple being married. They are present to give their support.

A silk scarf is wrapped around the hands of the bride and groom and they both eat from a silver bowl. This shows that they will now share everything.

During the service, they may make these promises to each other:

"I will love and respect my wife, be kind to her, always stay with her, give her presents and let her organize everything in the home."

"I will love my husband, look after our home, be careful with our money, welcome his friends and his family and always stay with him."

A newly married Buddhist couple may visit a temple to be blessed by the monks.

When the service is over the newly married couple will probably go to a local temple or monastery to be blessed by the monks and to pay respect to the Buddha.

Chinese

Presents for a Chinese wedding.

For Chinese people who follow the Taoist religion, a marriage has three different stages: the engagement, the wedding, and the welcoming of the bride into her husband's family.

First, a go-between arranges for a present to be sent from the bridegroom's family to the bride's family. If they accept the present, the horoscopes of the two people are checked to make sure they will be happy together. Next, they pray to the gods to ask them to bless the horoscopes.

The bridegroom's family then pay some money to the bride's family because they are losing a daughter. The gods are asked for a suitable day for the marriage to take place,

Both the bride and groom may wear silk costumes.

and the bride is welcomed into her future husband's family.

The wedding takes place at the home of the bridegroom. As the bride travels to the house, she drops a fan to show that she is no longer a daughter.

As the bride enters her new home, she cries because she is leaving her parents. During the service, many gifts and prayers are offered to the gods of the family, and also to

This Chinese bride is wearing a dress decorated with dragons, a sign of good luck. Sometimes costumes are decorated with a phoenix, also a symbol of good luck.

the gods of the house and the neighborhood, asking them to bless the wedding.

Christianity

Although there are many different groups of Christians, all their wedding ceremonies are very similar. The Anglican ceremony is described here.

First of all, the man and woman tell their families and friends that they are going to be married. This is called an engagement, and often people have a party to celebrate.

Next they arrange the date of the wedding with the priest or minister of the church in which they wish to be married. Each Sunday for three weeks before the wedding, banns are read aloud in most churches. These tell the members that the two people want to be married.

On the day of the wedding, the bridegroom arrives at the church with a friend, who is

At a Christian wedding, the bride usually wears a white dress, and the groom wears a suit.

The groom places a ring on the third finger of the bride's left hand.

called the best man. The bride arrives with her father. There is a tradition that the bride wears:

Something old, something new, something borrowed, something blue.

They all stand before the altar of the church. The bride's father gives her away to the bridegroom and the couple promise to love and look after each other. They ask God to help them to stay with each other until death parts them.

The clergyman blesses a ring, and the bridegroom places it on the third finger of the bride's left hand. Sometimes the bride gives a ring to the bridegroom.

After the service they leave the church, and their friends throw rice or pieces of colored paper, called confetti, over them.

There is a big party, or reception, and the guests give presents to the newly married couple. After this the bride and groom usually go away on their honeymoon, which is a vacation to celebrate their wedding.

Sometimes a couple may not wish to marry in a church. Couples can also be married at

In some countries, the bride and groom sign a marriage contract during the service.

a city or town hall by the mayor or a judge. The couple make a legal contract of marriage and sign a document, which binds them as husband and wife.

At the wedding reception, the bride and groom cut the wedding cake.

Hinduism

The day of a Hindu wedding is decided upon by the priest, who looks at the couple's horoscopes to find the most suitable time for the ceremony.

Before the service, the bride takes a bath, and her friends paint patterns on her hands and feet with an orange dye called henna.

The friends of a Hindu bride decorate her hands and feet with henna.

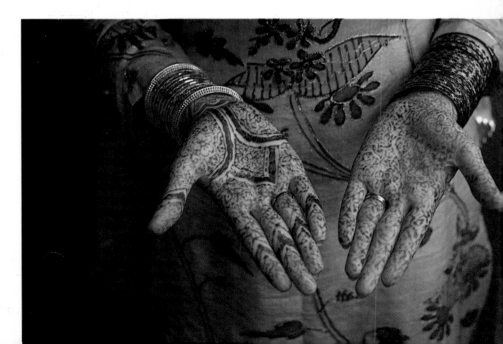

The bride wears a red sari decorated with gold thread to bring good fortune, and has gold jewelry on her wrists and ankles. Before the ceremony, the groom's family places a small mark of red paste on her forehead.

When they arrive at the entrance to the temple, the bride and groom both have veils over their faces.

A Hindu bride. The red mark on the bride's forehead is always worn by married women.

An image of Lord Ganesha, a Hindu god.

The ceremony begins with prayers to Lord Ganesha, a god with the head of an elephant. His aid is sought to bring success to all new projects. The couple sit in front of a sacred fire, facing each other under a canopy. The priest reads a list of their families and then says prayers.

A cord is placed over the couple's shoulders as a sign that they are joined together, and

the two people hold hands. After this they walk around the sacred fire seven times and make promises to each other and to the gods. The "walk" shows they will travel through life together.

Finally, prayers are said wishing them good luck for the future, and everyone shares a meal given by the bride's family.

The Hindu couple walk around the sacred fire seven times.

Islam

Most Muslim weddings are arranged by the parents of the couple. They suggest to the young people that they are suitable to marry each other.

Before the wedding, the two families exchange presents of materials and jewelry. The dowry, which the groom will pay to the bride's family and which becomes the bride's property, is arranged.

Most Muslim weddings take place at home. Many brides wear a *khameez* (tunic) and *shalwar* (pants), with a lot of gold jewelry. The groom may also wear *shalwar* and a *khameez*, with a garland of flowers, or he may wear a suit.

Before a wedding, the families of a Muslim couple exchange presents and arrange the dowry.

21

*A Muslim bride
wearing gold jewelry.*

On the day of the wedding, the bride and
groom do not meet until the ceremony is over.
They sit in separate rooms, the bride with
the female and the groom with the male
guests. A Muslim marriage is a simple prom-

ise to God made by the two people, but often the *Imam* (minister) is present. The bride says that she wishes to marry the groom, and he signs a marriage contract. After this they may both recite parts of the *Qur'an* (the Muslim holy book) and the *Imam* and the guests pray to *Allah* (God) to bless them.

After the wedding, the bride's family give a very large feast for everyone present.

The Muslim couple go to the feast given by the bride's family.

Judaism

A Jewish bride and groom stand together under the chuppah. *A wedding may take place wherever the* chuppah *is present.*

On the Sabbath (Saturday) before a Jewish wedding, the groom must go to the synagogue (where Jews worship) and read from the *Torah* (the holy book).

The groom and the rabbi read the marriage contract.

Jewish weddings are events of great celebration, and usually take place on a Sunday. The groom wears a dark suit and the bride wears white. They both stand with their parents under a *chuppah* (a canopy), which is usually put up in the synagogue. The canopy represents the couple's future home and happiness. The rabbi (the minister) pours a cup of wine and thanks God for marriages. Then the bride and groom share some of the wine and the marriage contract is read.

The groom places a plain gold ring on the first finger of the bride's left hand and tells everyone that she is his wife. Then he moves it to the third finger.

A second cup of wine is drunk and the rabbi says the *Seven Blessings*, which praise God and ask for happiness for the newly married couple.

The groom places a gold ring on the first finger of the bride's left hand, and then moves it to the third finger.

At the end of the ceremony, the groom breaks a small glass with his foot and the people shout *"Mazel tov!"* – "congratulations!" The breaking of the glass is a reminder of the destruction of the temple of Jerusalem. At moments of greatest joy there is always a little pain.

Afterwards, everyone goes to a party where they sing and dance with the bride and groom.

Sikhism

An engagement ceremony is held before a Sikh wedding. The bridegroom meets with the men of his and the bride's family, and they exchange gifts. A copy of the *Guru Granth Sahib* (the holy book) must be present.

The bride may have a similar meeting with the women of her family.

The ceremony usually takes place early in the morning at a *Gurdwara* (a Sikh temple). The groom sits in front of the *Guru Granth Sahib* and the bride joins him. She wears red clothes – either a *sari*, or *shalwar* and a *khameez*. Her feet and hands are painted with henna.

Any Sikh may conduct the ceremony. Prayers are said to ask God to bless the

A Sikh bride and groom wear colorful clothes.

27

couple, and the Sikh idea of marriage is explained to them.

The couple bow to the *Guru Granth Sahib* to show that they both agree to the marriage, and their scarves are tied together. Then they walk around the holy book while a hymn is

The couple sit before the Guru Granth Sahib, *the Sikh holy book.*

sung. Finally, *kara parshad* (a special food) is given to everyone present.

After the ceremony, all the guests share a meal. The couple first visit the bride's home and then go to the house where they will live together.

The couple's scarves are tied together.

Glossary

Altar The raised area at the front of a church, where religious ceremonies are performed.

Best man The friend of the bridegroom who accompanies him on the day of his wedding to the place where he is to be married.

Bride A woman on her wedding day.

Bridegroom or **groom** A man on his wedding day.

Buddha The founder of Buddhism.

Dragon A fabulous animal with wings and claws that usually breathes fire.

Horoscope A chart used to predict a person's future, comparing the positions of the planets, sun, and moon at the time of birth with their position at the time of the reading.

Phoenix A fabulous bird, said to set fire to itself and rise anew from the ashes.

Sabbath The Jewish holy day.

Sacred Dedicated to the worship of God or gods.

Sari A woman's dress.

Sponsors The couple who sit with the bride and groom at a Buddhist wedding ceremony.

Taoist A follower of Taoism, a Chinese religion and way of life.

Further Information

If you would like to find out more about the various religions discussed in this book, you may wish to read the following:

Eastern Religions by Elizabeth Seeger. Published by Crowell Jr. Bks.

Founders of Religion by Tony D. Triggs. Published by Silver Burdett Co.

Religions by James Haskins. Published by Lippincott Junior Bks. Group.

Six World Religions by L. Aletrino. Published by Morehouse-Barlow Co.

Videos

explain the role of the Protestant church in modern times.

Church Collection – helps to Includes the sacraments of Baptism and Holy Communion. 73 min. Produced by Family Films.

The Holy Koran – Islam's contributions to the world are examined. 60 min. Produced by Mastervision.

Holy Land and Holy City – a look at the Holy Land at Christmas and the activities of the Vatican during the reign of Pope Paul VI. 58 min. Produced by Mastervision.

The Message – the life of Muhammad, founder of the Islamic religion. 180 min. Produced by USA.

Acknowledgments

The Publisher would like to thank the following for providing the pictures for the book: Bruce Coleman 9, 18, 19; Bury and Ann Peerless 28; Camerapix Hutchison Library 8, 10, 13, 15, 27, 29; ICOREC 24, 25, 26; Macquitty International 5; Preben Christiansson 6, 12, 14, 20, 21; Zefa (cover), 16

Index